WORLD MYTHS AND LEGENDS II

Russia

Gus Gedatus

Fearon/Janus/Quercus
Belmont, CA

Simon & Schuster Education Group

World Myths and Legends

Greek and Roman
Ancient Middle Eastern
Norse
African
Far Eastern
Celtic
Native American
Regional American

World Myths and Legends II

India
Russia
Europe
South America
The Caribbean
Central America
Mexico
Southeast Asia

Series Editor: Joseph T. Curran
Cover Designer: Dianne Platner
Text Designer: Teresa A. Holden
Interior Illustrations: Mary Beth Gaitskill
Cover Photo: The Granger Collection, New York

Library of Congress Catalog Card Number: 92–72306
ISBN 0–8224–4647–2
Printed in the United States of America
2. 10 9 8 7 6 5 4 3 2 1
EB

CONTENTS

An Introduction to the Myths and Legends of Russia

Russia has given us hundreds of exciting folk legends. Many of these legends became popular with the Russian people very long ago. In fact, most legends were told many years before people started recording them in books. Teachers told them to their students, and parents told them to their children.

Russian legends include stories of great wars, with heroes and villains and much destruction. Hundreds of years ago, when these myths were first told, wars were common occurrences.

Animals play an important part in many of these tales. When they began to be told, people lived closer to nature. It was a time that people depended on animals in order to survive. In the stories, some animals help the hero through dangerous adventures. Other animals are magical beings that the hero tries to capture.

Russia is a land that has many rivers and lakes. In some of the myths, water plays an important part. At times people can be brought back to life if water is sprinkled on their dead bodies.

Witches appear in many Russian legends. The best-known witch is Baba Yaga. She lives deep in the forest in a little hut on chickens' legs. Russian peasants used to live in simple houses that were raised up on huge tree stumps with their roots attached. These stumps looked somewhat like a chicken's claw. Perhaps that is why Baba Yaga's hut is on chickens' legs.

Unlike the witches that appear in some stories, Baba Yaga doesn't ride a broom. When she travels, she rides a mortar, which looks like a shallow bowl. She steers with a pestle, a club-shaped tool. The pestle was used by people to pound or grind material, such as grain, in the mortar.

The characters of Ivan and Vasilisa appear in many stories. These names were common at the time many of the legends began. Ivan is still one of the most common Russian names. In the stories, a man named Ivan is usually strong and smart. A woman named Vasilisa is usually beautiful and has long, flowing hair.

In Russian legends, many people have magical powers. Some characters are able to change their shapes from human to animal form. Other people have superhuman strength and can perform wondrous acts that amaze everyone.

Many colorful monsters appear in Russian legends. There are dragons with many heads, fierce giants, and creatures hiding in the forest. Some of these creatures keep human prisoners, and stories are told of their eventual escape from these monsters.

Many Russians lived in areas surrounded by forests. Many stories have developed about the animals and other strange creatures that live there. Most of the tales in this book were told by peasants who lived far away from large cities. During the cold winter nights, these peasants kept warm around their wood-burning stoves. The stories they told then are the same stories that we read today.

The Firebird

In many Russian legends, animals help people who are in trouble. A very wise and powerful wolf is the animal who helps and advises the hero during this adventure. This hero is a tsar, a ruler of Russia.

The Unknown Thief

Long ago in a faraway country, Tsar Vladislas had a beautiful garden filled with the finest plants and trees. A tree that bore golden apples was his favorite. He was very proud of this tree. Every morning the tsar would stroll through the garden and count the apples. Each day he counted the same number.

One day, much to the tsar's surprise, he found that an apple was missing. The next day, another one was gone. Soon five of his precious golden apples had disappeared. The tsar was very upset, and he called for his three sons, Peter, Vasily, and Ivan.

"Hear me, my sons," the tsar proclaimed. "I want you to stand watch during the night to protect my golden apples. I will share my kingdom with the one who catches the thief." His sons agreed to take turns guarding the apple tree.

That night Peter sat down beside the apple tree. Soon he fell into a deep sleep. When he woke up the next morning, he counted the apples. Another golden apple had vanished.

The next night, Vasily sat down to protect the tree. Soon he, too, had fallen asleep. By morning one more apple was gone. The tsar threw up his hands.

"Don't worry, Father," Ivan, the youngest son, declared, "I'll catch the thief."

The third night, Ivan paced back and forth beneath the tree. He hummed and rubbed his eyes with dew to keep himself awake. In the early morning, Ivan saw a light from far away. It grew closer and brighter until a firebird landed in the tsar's apple tree.

It was the most beautiful bird Ivan had ever seen. Its feathers were gold, orange, and red. The brilliant colors sparkled in the sunlight.

Ivan watched as the bird began to pluck one of the golden apples. Then Ivan jumped high into the air and grabbed the bird by the

The firebird

tail. The firebird squawked, broke free of Ivan's grasp, and flew off. Ivan had only one of the bird's feathers in his hand. He was happy, though, that the bird had not taken another apple.

Ivan told the tsar that a firebird had been stealing the apples. The tsar was glad to find out who the thief had been. Once again, the tsar called his sons together.

"Hear me, my sons," the tsar said. "I want you to ride out into the world and capture the firebird. Remember my promise. Whoever catches this thief will share my kingdom."

The three brothers saddled their horses and left in search of the firebird.

The Meeting of Gray Wolf

Ivan rode day and night until he came to a stone pillar where three roads came together. A message was carved on the pillar. Ivan read the message aloud. "Whoever takes the path that lies straight ahead will get cold and hungry. Whoever takes the path on the right will see his horse die. Whoever takes the path on the left will die himself."

Ivan wanted to live, so he took the path to the right. Two days later, a gray wolf sprang out from some bushes and killed his horse.

Ivan didn't know what to do. He didn't think he could find the firebird on foot. Ivan walked for two days. On the third day, he sat down on an old tree stump. His head hung down. Then he looked up and saw the gray wolf again.

"What's wrong?" Gray Wolf asked. "Why are you so sad?"

"I'll never finish my journey on foot," Ivan replied.

"You must have read the pillar," Gray Wolf said. "You knew what would happen. I feel sorry for you, though. I killed your horse, so now I will be your servant. What are you doing here?"

"My father has sent me to catch the firebird who stole the golden apples," Ivan replied.

"Well," Gray Wolf said, "climb on my back. I'm the only one who knows where the firebird is."

Ivan climbed on Gray Wolf's back. Together they traveled across mountains, valleys, and oceans.

In a while, they came to a high wall.

"Climb over the wall and into the garden," Gray Wolf said. "There you will find the firebird in a golden cage. Take the firebird, but don't take the cage or you'll be in trouble."

Ivan climbed over the wall, found the firebird, and took it from its cage. Then he thought, "How will I carry this bird without a cage? Besides, the cage is covered with diamonds!" Ivan grabbed the cage. As he did so, loud bells rang. Then guards appeared and took Ivan to their master, Tsar Afron.

"I know you," Tsar Afron said. "You are Ivan, the son of Tsar Vladislas. If you had asked me for the firebird, I would have given it to you. Now I shall tell all the world that you are a thief."

Tsar Afron thought for a moment. Then he said, "If you do me a favor, though, I'll forgive you."

"What can I do, sir?" asked Ivan. Tsar Afron explained that he had always wanted the horse with a golden mane. This horse, he said, could be found in the stables of Tsar Kusman.

"Bring me that horse," Tsar Afron said. "Then I shall forgive you, and I will give you the firebird."

Ivan found Gray Wolf and told him what had happened. "Why didn't you do as I said?"

Gray Wolf asked. "I told you not to touch the firebird's cage."

"I'm sorry," Ivan said. "Forgive me." Then he climbed onto Gray Wolf and off they traveled over mountains and valleys.

When they arrived at Tsar Kusman's kingdom, Gray Wolf said, "Now climb over the wall. Take the horse with the golden mane, but don't touch the golden bridle. If you do, you'll be in trouble."

The stable guards were fast asleep as Ivan took the horse with the golden mane. He saw a golden bridle hanging on the wall.

"I must have this fine bridle," Ivan decided and touched it. Just as he touched it, loud bells began to ring, and the guards woke up. They grabbed Ivan and took him to Tsar Kusman.

"I have seen you before," Tsar Kusman said. "You are the son of Tsar Vladislas. Why did you steal my horse? If you had asked me for it, I would have given it to you. Now I will tell all the world that you are a thief."

The tsar stopped for a moment. "If you do something for me, though," he said, "I may forgive you."

"What do you want me to do?" Ivan asked.

"Go to the end of the earth," the tsar

continued, “and bring me Elena the Beautiful, daughter of Tsar Dalmat. Then I shall be so happy that I will give you the horse with the golden mane.”

Ivan returned to Gray Wolf. “I should have done as you told me,” Ivan said. “I’m sorry.” Then Ivan climbed once more onto Gray Wolf’s back, and the two traveled off together.

When they reached the kingdom of Tsar Dalmat, Gray Wolf said, “This time I’ll do it myself. You wait here.”

At midnight, Gray Wolf leapt over the fence and waited in the bushes for Elena the Beautiful. He waited all night and all the next day. In the early evening, Gray Wolf saw her walking in the garden. Gray Wolf jumped out of the bushes, picked her up, and carried her over the wall to Ivan.

“Ivan, get on my back!” Gray Wolf yelled. Ivan took Elena the Beautiful into his arms and jumped onto Gray Wolf’s back. Off they rode toward the palace of Tsar Kusman. Before they got there, Ivan started to feel very sad. He realized that he had fallen in love with the young maiden.

“I don’t want to take her back to marry that old tsar,” Ivan sadly told Gray Wolf. “I want to marry her myself!"

"Very well," Gray Wolf said, "I will help you again. I will make myself look like Elena. Then you can take me to the tsar in exchange for the horse."

Ivan hid Elena the Beautiful in a grove of trees. Then Gray Wolf rolled himself on the ground and turned into the exact image of the young maiden. They both walked up to the tsar's palace. When Tsar Kusman saw them, he joyfully gave Ivan the horse with the golden mane and the golden bridle. Ivan got on the horse and rode off to get Elena the Beautiful. Together they rode off to the kingdom of Tsar Afron.

Meanwhile, Tsar Kusman prepared to marry the look-alike Elena. Before the wedding was to take place, the bride wanted to take a walk alone in the garden. As soon as Gray Wolf was outside, he rolled on the ground and became himself once again. Then he caught up with Ivan, the real Elena, and the horse with the golden mane.

Gray Wolf noticed that Ivan looked sad. "What's wrong?" Gray Wolf asked.

"I don't want to give Tsar Afron this horse in exchange for the firebird," Ivan told Gray Wolf. "Can you make yourself look like the horse with the golden mane?"

"Of course," Gray Wolf replied. Ivan hid Elena and the horse. Gray Wolf rolled on the ground until he became another horse with a golden mane. Ivan jumped onto his back and rode off to Tsar Afron's palace. The grateful tsar thanked Ivan and gave him the firebird and the golden cage in exchange for the horse.

Ivan went back to Elena and the horse with the golden mane. Together Ivan, Elena the Beautiful, and the firebird rode off on the horse toward Ivan's home.

The next morning, Tsar Afron tried out his new horse. He ran after a fox and was pleased with how fast the horse could run. Suddenly the horse vanished and Gray Wolf appeared. When the tsar realized he was riding a wolf, he lost his balance and fell to the ground.

Gray Wolf soon caught up to the young couple. "This is the place where I killed your horse, Ivan," Gray Wolf said. "Now I will no longer be your servant."

"Good-bye, Gray Wolf," Ivan replied. "Thank you for everything."

"Oh, you'll see me again," Gray Wolf answered.

The Brothers' Revenge

Ivan, Elena the Beautiful, the firebird, and the horse with the golden mane rode on a bit more. They were very tired and stopped for a rest. Soon they were fast asleep.

Ivan's brothers found them asleep on the ground.

"Ivan has made us look foolish," Peter said. "First he grabs that bird's feather. Next he finds the firebird. Then he meets this beautiful maiden. Now he has a horse with a golden mane."

"We should teach him a lesson," Vasily exclaimed. Then both the brothers drove swords through Ivan, killing him. The noise woke Elena, who began to scream.

"Be quiet and do as we say," Peter shouted at Elena as he put his sword to her heart. "You must tell our father that we won your favor. You must say that we found the firebird and the horse with the golden mane. You will be my bride, and my brother will keep the horse."

Gray Wolf's Last Appearance

Soon after the brothers and Elena had left, a crow flew down and sat on Ivan's body. Suddenly Gray Wolf appeared. He saw the crow and grabbed it in his jaws.

"Fly to the end of the earth and bring back the magic water of life," Gray Wolf said to the crow. The crow flew away. In a short while, it returned with a bottle of water tied to its leg. Gray Wolf sprinkled the magic water over Ivan's body. Soon the young man came back to life.

Gray Wolf then explained to Ivan all that had happened. Ivan became very angry with his brothers. Then he hopped on Gray Wolf's back and rode to his father's kingdom.

Outside the walls of the palace, Gray Wolf said, "Good-bye, Ivan. Hurry. There is no time to lose!"

Ivan entered the palace just as the wedding of Peter and Elena was about to begin. Ivan's brothers fainted when they saw him. Elena ran to Ivan and embraced him. She stepped forward and spoke to Tsar Vladislas.

"This is the man who won my heart," she said to Ivan's father. "I want him to be my husband."

Elena told the tsar the whole story. After hearing what evil things his two older sons had done, the tsar sent them away forever. He proclaimed Ivan the heir to his kingdom.

Ivan and Elena got married that day. They often told the story of Gray Wolf to their children and grandchildren.

1. *How did Ivan stay awake under the apple tree?*
2. *Why did Gray Wolf become Ivan's servant?*
3. *Why did Ivan get into so much trouble?*

Emilyan and the Pike

Some Russian folktales contain a simple message about the character flaws in people. In this story, a fish helps a selfish peasant boy become a kind man.

Emilyan Meets the Pike

A selfish and lazy young man named Emilyan lived with his mother in a village beside the Volga River. All day long he would play games instead of helping the poor woman.

"Emilyan!" his mother shouted one day. "Stop playing right now and go outside to get us some water from the river. Chopping through the winter ice is hard work for an old woman like me."

Emilyan grumbled as he picked up the water buckets on their wooden yoke. He put the yoke on his shoulders and then picked up an axe. Emilyan walked to the river, still grumbling.

"I hate doing this," he complained as he whacked away at the ice. "It's cold out here."

When Emilyan had chopped a big hole

through the ice, he lowered the buckets into the river. He filled the buckets with water and then pulled them out of the river and onto the ice.

When Emilyan looked into the buckets, he had a big surprise. He had caught a beautiful pike!

"Oh, what luck!" Emilyan exclaimed. "I'll have this for dinner."

"No!" the pike cried out. "I must return to the sea! Please! Put me back in the river. If you do, I will grant you many wishes."

"How could a fish help me?" Emilyan asked.

"I'm no ordinary fish," the pike said. "Have you ever heard a fish talk before?"

"Well, no," said Emilyan, "I suppose not."

"If you put me back in the river, you'll never have to work again," the pike added.

Suddenly Emilyan was very interested. "Tell me more," he said.

The pike said, "I can make these heavy water buckets carry themselves home. From now on, whenever you want any work done, this is all you need to do. Say 'By my wish and at the pike's command.' Then whatever you want will be done. Now be a good fellow and let me go."

"Oh, all right," Emilyan said. He dumped the fish back into the river. Emilyan watched the pike go. Then he tried to lift the yoke. It was quite heavy.

"The pike's words probably won't work," he thought, "but I might as well give them a try. Go home, water buckets. By my wish and at the pike's command, go home." Then the yoke and the buckets rose into the air and began to float off! Emilyan followed happily behind them.

"It works!" he shouted. "I'm glad I didn't eat that fish."

The next day Emilyan's mother asked him to chop firewood. Emilyan was about to complain when he remembered the pike's promise.

"I'll try this again," he thought. "Wood, by my wish and at the pike's command, get yourself split and make a pile near the fireplace."

At once the wood was split and stacked. The pike's words had worked again.

Emilyan found that he could use the magic words to get his chores done. He was happy because he had much more time to play. His mother was thrilled because the chores got done.

The yoke and the buckets float off

Emilyan Meets a Princess

One day Emilyan's mother asked him to go into the village. Emilyan went out to the barn. He wrapped himself in a blanket and sat down in the sled. He spoke the pike's magic words, and the sled sped off.

His mother watched at a window. "Why, Emilyan is driving the sled without a horse!" she exclaimed.

With the pike's help, Emilyan rode the horseless sled into town. Many people saw him pass. "Emilyan is a magician!" they shouted to one another. "We thought he was selfish and lazy."

Soon the news of Emilyan's power spread throughout the land. It reached the tsar in his great palace on the Caspian Sea. The tsar called for the young man.

When Emilyan got the tsar's message, he used the magic words again. "By my wish and at the pike's command, take me to the tsar's palace," he said. At that, he was whisked away.

When Emilyan reached the palace, he greeted the tsar this way: "Hey, tsar old boy. You called for me?"

The tsar turned purple with anger. How dare this peasant talk to him like that! The tsar was so angry that he wanted to have Emilyan killed. First, though, he had to find out the secret of his magic. Emilyan, however, would not tell his secret.

The tsar came up with a plan. He called for his beautiful daughter, Natasha. He thought that Natasha could charm Emilyan into telling his secret.

Natasha and Emilyan began spending lots of time together. They talked and laughed and played games. Natasha grew very fond of Emilyan, but Emilyan was not charmed. Emilyan felt that Natasha was good company, but he did not really care for her beyond that.

"Oh, Father," sighed Natasha one day, "I think Emilyan is a wonderful man. I want to marry him."

This had not been part of the tsar's plan. He was furious, but Natasha would not change her mind.

"Oh, very well," the tsar replied. "You may marry the young man." The tsar was sure that once they were married, Emilyan would tell Natasha of his magic power.

The Change

On the day of the marriage, Emilyan

acted in a very foolish way. He talked and laughed during the wedding. He ate with his fingers and made strange noises at dinner.

The tsar was truly embarrassed.

"I don't care if he does have magic powers," the tsar cried. "I can't have this rude clown in the royal family. I must get rid of him!" So the tsar had a sleeping potion added to Emilyan's wine. As soon as the young man was fast asleep, the tsar called to his guards.

"Seal this man in a barrel and throw him out to sea," the tsar said to the guards.

When Natasha tried to stop them, the tsar had her sent away. She was taken to an island not far from the palace.

"Maybe someday the girl will come to her senses," the tsar said.

For many days, Natasha sat in a dirty hut on the island. Every day she cried for Emilyan.

Meanwhile, Emilyan went rolling over the waves in his barrel. After many days, he woke up dazed and afraid. Then he heard a familiar voice.

"Emilyan, this is your friend, the pike," yelled the fish. "You are floating at sea. Your wife sits crying in a lowly hut on an island.

What would you like me to do?"

"Throw this barrel on the shore near my wife," said Emilyan. "Then let me out of it. I must help Natasha."

This was the first time in his life that Emilyan had wanted to help someone else.

The pike said, "I am very pleased with you, Emilyan."

The pike took the barrel to the shore of Natasha's island. Then he made the barrel split open. Natasha saw all this and came running to her husband.

Natasha's dress was torn, her face was dirty, and her eyes were red from crying. Emilyan, however, saw Natasha in a new way. She looked ragged and dirty, but she was also beautiful. Emilyan fell deeply in love with the young princess.

"Don't cry, my wife," he said. "By my wish and at the pike's command, make this hut a palace." The little hut became a gold and marble palace that was filled with many riches. A crystal bridge appeared. It led from the island to the palace of the tsar.

The young couple made peace with the tsar. Then Emilyan sent a messenger to bring his mother to visit them in their golden palace. He also had a huge cake made and a keg filled with fine wine. He sent these out to sea as presents for the pike.

Emilyan and Natasha lived happily on their island. They stayed there until the tsar died. Then they moved to the tsar's palace and became the kingdom's rulers. They were kind rulers. Emilyan never forgot what he had learned from the pike. Emilyan realized that helping people was better than thinking only of himself.

1. *How could Emilyan first tell that the pike was different from other fish?*
2. *Why did the tsar agree to let his daughter marry Emilyan?*
3. *In what way did Emilyan change?*

Finist the Falcon

Some Russian stories are like stories from other countries. This story might remind you of the story you know as "Cinderella" or of "Beauty and the Beast."

An Unusual Present

Once upon a time, there was an old man who had three daughters. The two older daughters never thought of anything but fine clothes and jewels. Mary, the youngest daughter, did all of the cooking and cleaning.

Mary was very beautiful and very good. She had a bright, smiling face, and she always had kind words for everyone.

One day the father was going to market. He always brought presents from the market for his daughters. He asked his three daughters what presents they would like.

The two older girls wanted fine silk for making new dresses.

"Mary, what shall I bring you?" the father asked.

Mary had an unusual request to ask her father. "I want a feather of Finist the Bright

Falcon," she replied immediately.

The father agreed to try to find what his daughters wanted. He rode off to the market.

At the market, the man bought two rolls of fine silk for the older daughters. He looked for a feather from the falcon but could not find one.

Just outside of town he met an old man carrying a little box.

"What have you got there, good sir?" the father asked.

"A feather of Finist the Bright Falcon," the old man answered.

The father was surprised and happy. He would be able to please his youngest daughter after all. He gave the old man a thousand rubles for the box with the feather in it. Then he rode home and gave the presents to his three happy daughters. Mary held the little box close to her heart.

That night, when they had all finished supper, Mary went to her room and opened the box. The beautiful feather dropped to the floor.

"Finist the Bright Falcon, come to me," Mary whispered.

Suddenly there was a handsome prince where the falcon feather had been! Mary was afraid at first. Then the prince spoke to her.

"You are my beloved," the prince said. "I'll fly near your window every night. If you ever need anything, wave the feather in the air and you shall have it. Wave it again and it will disappear." He kissed her.

The next moment the prince became a bird once again and flew off into the forest.

The prince came back to see Mary every night for many weeks.

Mary's Mistake

Every week Mary's sisters would go off to fancy teas and to church on Sunday. They wore the new silk dresses they had made. Since Mary did not have silk dresses, she did not go with her sisters. She would wait until they were gone, and then she would wave the feather in the air.

By waving the feather, Mary could have her own fine new dress. She could also have sparkling jewels. Then she would go off to the places where her sisters had gone. Often Mary would see her sisters at parties, but they didn't know her. She looked so very different from the girl they had left at home.

One night when Mary came home, she forgot to take off one of her jewels. It was a shining diamond pin. When her sisters came home, they saw the pin and knew that something was very strange.

The sisters waited outside her bedroom door and heard Mary talking to someone. Then the oldest sister saw Finist flying out of the window. The sisters decided to find out what was going on.

The next night, the mean sisters climbed a ladder by Mary's window. They placed sharp knives all around the open window. That night Finist could not get in the window. He tore his wings on the sharp knives when he tried to get in.

"Good-bye, Mary," he called out. "If you want me, you will have to walk to the other side of the earth."

Mary cried when she heard Finist say these words. She cried all night long and all the next day. Then she decided what she had to do.

Mary told her father that she would have to take a very long trip. At last he agreed. Mary set out through the dark forests.

Mary's Long Trip

Mary climbed high mountains and swam across angry seas. She walked through dark

Finist flies away

forests and across burning deserts. She searched everywhere for Finist the Bright Falcon.

After searching for a long time, Mary came to a strange little hut on chickens' legs. The hut was spinning around and around.

"Stay still, little hut," Mary begged. "Turn your door toward me. I want to come in." The hut stopped spinning, and Mary went inside. On the floor, she found a witch with bony legs and a huge nose.

"Foo!" the witch snorted. "Here is a pretty young Russian woman! What are you looking for, my dear?"

Mary told the witch about Finist the Bright Falcon. The witch knew about him. She told Mary that Finist would be married the very next day. Then she gave Mary a golden egg on a silver saucer.

"When you roll this egg on this plate, you will have countless more golden eggs. You can use it to win the favor of Finist's wife, the princess. Then you may see Finist the Bright Falcon. Now go and see my sister witch."

Mary found another hut and the sister witch inside it. This witch told Mary that Finist had already married the princess. She gave Mary a silver loom and a golden needle and sent her on her way.

Soon Mary came to a wide sea. On the opposite shore, she could see the white domes and towers of a palace. With her presents tied in a cloth on her arm, Mary swam to the faraway shore. There she began working on the silver loom.

The princess came out of the palace to watch Mary work.

"Would you sell me your loom?" the princess asked.

Mary replied, "If you let me see Finist the Bright Falcon, I will give it to you."

The princess took the loom back home with her. She planned to let Mary visit Finist but only when he was sleeping. That night she gave Finist a sleeping potion. Then she led Mary to his room.

Mary stood by Finist's bed and cried, "Finist the Bright Falcon, it's Mary! I've walked through forests and over deserts. I've climbed high mountains and swum angry seas. Now I've found you at last. Wake up!" Finist did not wake up. Soon the princess came back, and Mary had to leave the palace.

The next day Mary sat on the shore

rolling the golden egg on the saucer. Many more golden eggs appeared. The princess wanted the golden eggs. Mary said she would give the princess the golden eggs if she could see Finist again. The princess agreed.

The princess once more gave Finist a sleeping potion.

That night at the bedside, Mary called to Finist again. "Finist the Bright Falcon, it's Mary. I've walked through forests and over deserts. I've climbed high mountains and swum across angry seas. Now I have found you. Wake up!"

Finist did not wake up. The princess came back and led the sad girl away as before.

On the third day, Mary sewed gleaming dresses with the golden needle. Again, the princess made a trade with Mary. She let Mary in to see Finist in order to have the needle for her own.

"Finist the Bright Falcon, it's Mary," she said. She went on as she had on the past two nights. Finist kept sleeping because of the sleeping potion.

Mary began to cry once again. She reached over the sleeping bird to hug him. Then one of her tears fell onto his cheek.

Finist woke up and looked at Mary.

Mary told Finist about her sisters and the witches and her long, terrible travels. Then she told him about the presents she had given the princess in order to see him. Finist the Bright Falcon still loved Mary. Hearing how she had found him made Finist love Mary more than ever.

Finist was angry with the princess. He called all of the wise people in the kingdom. He told them about Mary.

"What do you people think?" Finist asked. "Should I stay here with the one who sold me for silver and gold? Or should I be with the one who traveled through forests, up mountains, and over seas to find me?"

All the people agreed that Finist should be with the one who had given so much of herself. The selfish princess was sent away forever.

Mary and Finist the Bright Falcon were married. Everyone celebrated. Mary and Finist lived very happily ever after.

1. *How did Mary get the magic feather?*
2. *Who gave Mary the silver loom?*
3. *What caused Finist to finally wake up and see Mary?*

The Frog Princess

Some characters in Russian folktales change from humans to animals, plants, or objects. In this story, a frog has many special powers, including the ability to change into a beautiful woman.

A tsar once had three sons. When they grew up, the tsar called them to his chambers.

"It's time for you to get married," the tsar announced. "Take your bows to the field outside the palace walls. Shoot arrows into the air. Wherever your arrow lands you will find the woman you will marry."

The three sons liked this idea, so they carried their bows to the field. The oldest son shot an arrow to the right. The next oldest son shot to the left. The youngest son tried to shoot straight ahead, but his arrow curved in many directions.

The three brothers looked for their arrows. Lovely women picked up the arrows of the older brothers. The women gave the arrows to the brothers, who brought the women home to their father. The next day a grand wedding feast was held.

The youngest brother searched and searched but couldn't find his arrow. After three days, he came to a swamp, where he saw a little hut made of reeds. There was a large frog sitting in the open door of the hut. Ivan's arrow was in the frog's mouth.

The frog asked, "Prince Ivan, don't you want your arrow? You must come inside to get it."

The frog hopped up twice, and the tiny hut turned into a pretty little house. The young prince went inside. Again the frog hopped up twice, and a table full of food appeared. Ivan sat down and ate his fill.

"I am the one you must marry," the frog exclaimed. Ivan was confused, but he agreed. The next moment the frog changed into a beautiful woman. On the ground nearby lay her frog skin.

"During the day I will remain a frog," she explained, "but late at night I will be as you see me now."

In a few minutes, the woman became a frog once again. Ivan gently put her in a box and returned home.

The tsar was pleased to see his youngest son. The two older brothers and their wives

Ivan and the frog princess

laughed when they heard Ivan was going to marry a frog. However, the tsar agreed to it, and another wedding was held.

Ivan and the frog princess lived happily for some time. Then one day, the tsar called all his sons together.

"My sons," the tsar said, "I want each of your wives to make me a shirt." He gave each of his sons a piece of silk. "The shirts must be finished by tomorrow."

Ivan was very worried as he told the frog princess what she had to do. She, however, told Ivan not to worry at all.

The frog princess cut the piece of silk. When she had finished, she called out, "Summer winds, carry this cloth away and sew a shirt for my husband's father." In the morning, a beautiful shirt was ready for Ivan to take to his father.

Ivan and his brothers gave the shirts to their father. The tsar said, "The shirt made by Ivan's wife is the finest of them all. Now go back to your wives and have them weave me a carpet." He gave each son threads of silver and gold.

Ivan returned to his wife with word of his father's newest wish. She told him not to worry. Then she asked Ivan to leave her alone so that she could work.

"Summer winds," the frog princess called, "take these threads of silver and gold and make a carpet for my husband's father." In the morning, a beautiful carpet was ready for Ivan's father.

The brothers gave the carpets to their father. First he looked at the carpet made by the oldest son's wife. Then he looked at the carpet made by the second son's wife.

"These carpets are fit for me to wipe my boots on," the tsar said. Then he looked at the carpet made by the youngest son's wife. "This carpet will be put beneath my throne."

After that, the tsar told his sons to have each of their wives bake him a loaf of bread. This time the two older brothers sent a spy to see what Ivan's wife was doing.

The spy saw the frog princess turn into a woman. Then he saw her mix flour and water and put her bread dough into a cold oven. "Heat of nature," she said, "bake this bread."

The brothers' spy sent word to the other wives. They then tried to bake their bread in the same way. One wife's bread was burned to a crisp, and the other wife's bread was not baked at all.

"Ivan, your wife has baked the tastiest bread on all the earth," the tsar said. "I will have a royal banquet to honor her."

Ivan returned to the frog princess and told her about the banquet. He was worried about showing his wife to so many people.

"Everything will be well," the frog princess said. "Don't worry. You go first, and I'll come later."

The following night Ivan rode to the palace alone. His brothers and their wives were already there.

"Where is your beautiful wife?" the oldest brother teased Ivan. Then everyone began to laugh.

Later a grand carriage arrived at the palace gate. The frog princess, now a beautiful young woman in splendid clothes, joined Ivan at the banquet table.

The guests began to eat a delicious dinner. During dinner, Ivan's wife poured some wine into one sleeve of her dress. Then she dropped leftover roast duck bones down the other sleeve. The wives of the older brothers, seeing her do this, did the same thing.

After dinner the wives of the two older brothers waved their arms as they danced.

They sprayed wine from their sleeves and hit other guests with flying bones. The tsar was furious.

Soon after, Ivan's wife waved her arms, too. The wine from her sleeve became a crystal blue lake in the palace court. The bones turned into seven white swans.

While his wife was working her magic at the palace, Ivan went home and found the frog skin. He quickly burned it, hoping that his beautiful wife would never again use it.

"What have you done?" his wife asked when she returned home. "Now I must go far away. You will never see me again unless you come to the land of eternal sunlight." Then she turned into a swan and flew out the window.

Ivan began to cry. He didn't know how to find the land of eternal sunlight. He began the journey anyway. He swam rivers, scaled mountains, and roamed thick forests in search of this land. After many weeks, he found an old witch in a little hut on chickens' legs. He told her his sad story.

"I must find the land of eternal sunlight," Ivan told the witch.

"Don't worry about that," the witch said. "Your wife flies here every day to visit me.

When she comes, you must hold her tightly. She may change shapes, from a frog to a snake to a great crawling bug. You must not let her go. Then she will turn herself into an arrow. You must break the arrow over your knee. Only then will she be yours forever."

Ivan's wife visited the witch that day. When his wife started changing shapes, Ivan became too frightened to hold her. He then continued on his journey until he met another witch.

"Your wife flies here every day to visit me," said this witch. "When she comes, you must hold her tightly. She may change shapes, from a frog to a snake to a crawling bug. You must not let her go. Then she will become an arrow. Break that arrow over your knee. She will then be yours forever."

Again his wife came to visit. Again Ivan became afraid when she changed shapes.

"I wonder how much you really do love your wife," the witch said. Ivan continued on with his journey.

Soon Ivan met a third witch. She told him the same thing that the other witches had. This time when his wife came to visit, he acted differently.

His wife changed into a frog and then into

a snake and then into a great crawling bug. Ivan held on to her until she became an arrow. Then he took the arrow and broke it over his knee.

"Dear Ivan!" exclaimed his wife. "I will now be yours forever."

That day Ivan and his wife returned to his father's kingdom. His father held a banquet in their honor. All the people in the kingdom came to the banquet and met Ivan's beautiful wife. She never became a frog again.

1. *How did Ivan first meet the frog princess?*
2. *What did the two older brothers' wives do at the tsar's ball?*
3. *Who helped Ivan find his wife after she had changed into a swan and flown out the window?*

The Hero and the Dragon

One creature often found in Russian folktales is a huge, fire-breathing dragon with many heads. Such creatures were said to live in mountain caves. The grass outside the caves would burst into flames whenever a dragon walked there. In this story, one brave young man decides to fight a fire-breathing dragon.

Many years ago, a fierce mother dragon kept invading towns and carrying people to her cave. A young knight named Dobrynya, afraid for himself and his neighbors, killed many of the dragon's babies. He didn't want them to grow up to help their evil mother. He also wanted to rescue the prisoners in the dragon's cave.

"After what you've done," warned Dobrynya's own mother, "you must never go back to the mountain where the dragon lives. You must also stay away from her river."

Dobrynya didn't listen to his mother. The next day he went back to the mountains looking for other dragons to kill. When he got to the river near the mountain, he went for a swim. As soon as Dobrynya had jumped into the water, he saw sparks and great clouds of smoke. Before he could move, an ugly dragon with twelve heads appeared.

"Well, well, young Dobrynya, now I have you," the dragon roared. "Should I eat you here or take you back to my cave?"

Dobrynya jumped out of the river. He had no sword with which to defend himself.

"I think my end is near," he said quietly. Then he saw a hat lying on the shore. He thought that the hat might make a good weapon. So he picked it up and found that it was very heavy.

As the dragon swooped down to grab him, the young knight threw the hat into the air. In one great stroke, the hat knocked off most of the dragon's heads. The dragon fell to the ground. Dobrynya picked up the hat and held it over the dragon's chest.

"No, brave knight," the dragon begged, "let us be friends. I'll stop carrying off your people, and you stop killing my babies."

While Dobrynya was thinking about this, the dragon slipped out from beneath him and flew away. Dobrynya didn't know that the dragon was flying straight to Dobrynya's hometown for another prisoner.

When Dobrynya returned home, he was

The fierce mother dragon

called by Prince Vladimir to the royal palace.

"That wicked mother dragon has stolen my niece Zabava," the prince said. "Bring her back to me, and I will reward you greatly. Fail, and I will have you put to death."

Dobrynya went home and told his mother what had happened. She gave him a beautiful chestnut-colored horse and a magical silken whip.

"Have courage, my son," she told him. "Use the whip carefully, for it holds very special powers."

Dobrynya said good-bye to his mother. Then he mounted the chestnut horse and traveled over mountains and valleys. Soon the horse became weak. Along the way, baby dragons had bitten its legs.

Dobrynya pulled out the silken whip and whisked the horse between the ears. Then the horse became powerful again. Suddenly the mother dragon appeared.

"Dragon," Dobrynya screamed, "you broke our pact. Now give me back the princess Zabava."

The brave Dobrynya fought the dragon for three days and three nights. Dobrynya became so tired that he was just about to give up. Then he heard a voice from above.

"Fight for three more hours, Dobrynya," said the voice, "and you will win."

As Dobrynya continued fighting, the dragon led him to a valley near her cave. There stood the lovely princess Zabava. When Dobrynya saw the princess, he fought even harder. The dragon soon fell with a great crash.

"You have saved me!" the princess exclaimed.

Now, however, the dragon's blood was filling the valley so quickly that Dobrynya feared they would both drown. Then he heard another voice.

"Strike your sword into Mother Earth, Dobrynya, and speak your wish to her," the voice said.

Dobrynya struck his sword into the earth. "Please, Mother Earth," he begged, "swallow the blood of this foul dragon."

In a great rush, the blood disappeared into the earth.

Dobrynya returned Princess Zabava to her uncle, Prince Vladimir. The people who had been kept prisoners in the dragon's cave were all set free. The people never feared for their lives again, for the wicked dragon was at last dead.

1. *What did Dobrynya use to knock off most of the dragon's heads?*
2. *What did Dobrynya's mother give him before he rode off to fight the dragon?*
3. *How did Dobrynya stop the dragon's blood?*

The Bravery of Ivan the Pea

Here is another story about a very strong hero whose destiny is to fight a fierce dragon. This dragon was half serpent and half human.

A tsar and his wife had two sons and a beautiful daughter. For twenty years, the daughter lived in her room at the top of a high tower. She was never allowed outside, so no knight had ever seen her. She had long, golden hair, wound in a braid that reached down to her feet. The tsar called her Vasilisa of the Golden Braid.

One day the tsar sent word that Vasilisa was ready to choose a husband. All the single men in the kingdom were eager to meet the beautiful woman.

When Vasilisa heard the news, she was pleased. She longed more than ever to see the world outside her room. Vasilisa begged the tsar to let her spend one afternoon in the palace garden. The tsar agreed.

The young woman sat on the grass watching butterflies. Then she walked over to a small hill and picked flowers.

All of a sudden, a great wind blew into

the garden. It made the young woman laugh. Then it lifted her up and carried her through the sky over many lands. Vasilisa's parents saw her being carried away, but they could do nothing to get her back. Vasilisa landed, very gently, at the palace of a fierce dragon.

Vasilisa's parents were heartbroken. The tsar sent his two sons to search until they found their beautiful sister.

The brothers set out on their journey and traveled for two years. They had passed through many kingdoms when they saw a high mountain range in the distance. This was the home of the fierce dragon.

As they came nearer to the mountains, the brothers saw an old man at the side of the road. They gave him a silver coin and asked if he had seen their sister.

"Our master is a fierce dragon," the old man said. "He won't let us tell anyone how a great wind blew a beautiful young woman to this land."

The brothers guessed that their sister was near. They rode on until they came to a golden palace. Vasilisa saw her brothers through her window as they came into view. She cried out with joy when she recognized them. Then she called a servant to her side.

The servant secretly brought the brothers into the palace.

Soon the walls of the palace began to shake, and its roof began to glow. Vasilisa knew that this meant the dragon was near.

"Hide!" Vasilisa cried to her brothers. They quickly hid themselves behind a couch.

The dragon flew in with a great roar and a whistle. Then he called out, "I smell men. Where are you hiding, men?"

"We have come to rescue our sister," the brothers said, coming out of their hiding place.

With one of his wings, the dragon picked up the first brother. With his other wing, he picked up the second brother. Then he slammed the two men together, killing them both. He threw their bodies into a deep pit.

Vasilisa began to cry. For days she did not sleep or eat. Then she decided that she had to try to escape.

"Sweet dragon," she cooed, "you are so big and strong. I am sure that no one could ever defeat you."

"Some people say, my dear," replied the dragon, "that there is only one person who could beat me. He is supposedly called Ivan the Pea, but he'll never come!"

The dragon laughed, because he didn't believe there would ever be such a person. The dragon sent the young woman back to her chamber. She stayed there for ten years.

During that time, Vasilisa's mother thought about her daughter and sons every day. She had lost all her children. She spent many days roaming the woods. One day she stopped to fill a golden cup with water from a little stream. As she drank the water, she swallowed a tiny pea, which was at the bottom of the cup.

The pea grew and grew inside her. In time, Vasilisa's mother gave birth to a fine son. She named him Ivan the Pea.

As Ivan the Pea grew, he became very strong and as round as a pea. By the age of ten, he had grown as strong as a powerful warrior. One day his parents told him the story of how his sister had been blown away on a great wind.

"I beg you, Mother and Father," Ivan the Pea said, "let me go and find them." His parents thought he was too young, but finally they agreed.

Ivan rode his horse for two days until he came to a dark forest. There he saw a most unusual sight. A little wooden hut sat on chickens' legs. The hut was spinning around in the wind. Ivan went up to the hut.

"Hut, hut, I am Ivan the Pea," he sang. "Hut, hut, turn your door to me!" The hut stopped spinning, and an old witch stepped out. Ivan asked the witch if she had seen a great wind.

"That great wind was the power of a fierce dragon," the witch replied. "That dragon would eat you sooner than I would."

"How can I find this dragon?" Ivan asked.

"I will tell you," the witch said. "First you must agree to do something for me. Bring me some of the magical water the dragon has in his palace. It will make me young again."

Ivan agreed. Then the witch told him how to get to the dragon's palace.

Ivan traveled many more days until he came to the beggar his brothers had met many years before. The beggar told Ivan about the great wind and pointed to the range of mountains in the distance. Ivan knew his sister was near.

When Ivan approached the palace, Vasilisa was looking out her window. She wondered who he was and sent a servant to find out. When she discovered that Ivan was her youngest brother, she called out to him,

The witch's hut

warning him of the dragon.

"My sister," cried Ivan, "I am not afraid of a dragon. I am Ivan the Pea!"

Ivan entered the palace and sat down in the dragon's chair. Vasilisa gasped as the chair creaked beneath him.

"My goodness!" she exclaimed. "If you make that huge chair creak, you must be very, very strong!"

Ivan left the palace and went to the court blacksmith. The blacksmith made Ivan an iron staff that was too heavy for five grown men to lift. Ivan tossed the staff into the air and then caught it. He returned to his sister at the dragon's palace.

Soon Ivan and Vasilisa heard the whistle and roar of the dragon. This time the palace did not shake, for the powerful Ivan the Pea was holding it still.

The dragon entered his palace. When he saw Ivan, he grunted, "Could it be Ivan the Pea who has come to visit?"

"I am the one who will destroy you," Ivan said without fear.

"I will crush you with my dragon wings!" the dragon boomed.

"I don't think so," Ivan replied.

With all his might, Ivan the Pea hurled

his great staff at the dragon. It smashed the fiery monster into millions of pieces, which flew off into the sky. The staff flew out of the window and fell with a loud thud, disappearing deep into the earth.

Ivan searched the palace and found the magical water. Then he went to the deep pit where his brothers had been thrown. He sprinkled some water over their bodies. Suddenly they came back to life and thanked their brave brother for saving them.

The three brothers and Vasilisa traveled back to their homeland. They stopped on the way to give some of the magical water to the old witch. She became young once again.

Ivan's father and mother told the people in the town that their daughter had been found. The people were very happy. Soon Vasilisa found a husband, and Ivan found a wife. They were all married on the same day in their father's palace. After his father died, Ivan became the tsar. He ruled his people fairly for the rest of his life.

1. *How was Vasilisa brought to the dragon's palace?*
2. *How did the two brothers die?*
3. *How did Ivan the Pea bring his brothers back to life?*

Alesha Meets a Giant

This Russian tale introduces a giant named Tugarin, who meets his fate at the hands of a famous knight. This giant is not only huge in size but acts in a crude and rough way. He offends people with his lack of civilized habits.

A brave young knight named Alesha rode to the town of Kiev. He wanted to fight in Prince Vladimir's Army. On reaching the palace of the prince, Alesha was eager to announce himself.

"My name is Alesha," he said when he met the prince, "son of Leontii of Rostov."

"I have heard of you, Alesha," Prince Vladimir replied. "I am pleased that you are here. You would honor me if you took a place at my dinner table."

Alesha didn't think he was worthy enough to sit at the table with the prince and his wife. Instead, he climbed to a small ledge over the stove, a place where humble servants usually sat. From the ledge he could watch everything, without having to know royal table manners.

After Alesha had taken his seat on the

ledge, the door to the palace kitchen flew open. A giant as wide as two oak trees barged in. This giant was Tugarin.

Because he was a beast with no manners, Tugarin rudely sat down between the prince and his wife. Alesha saw all this and simply had to speak.

"Prince Vladimir, how can you let this beast sit between you and your wife?" Alesha asked. The prince was afraid of Tugarin and so said nothing.

Dinner was soon brought in, starting with roast duck. The monstrous Tugarin picked up the whole duck in his huge hand and ate it in one giant gulp. He chewed quickly and then spit the bones on the floor. Once again Alesha had to speak.

"My father once had a dog," Alesha said, "that choked to death on a duck's bone. I hope Tugarin does, too."

A large pie was the next course. The giant put his face into the center of the pie and slurped it up in a flash.

"My father once had a cow," Alesha said. "It sucked up some rocks from the earth and choked to death. I hope Tugarin does, too."

Tugarin became annoyed with Alesha's remarks and turned to the prince.

Tugarin the giant

"Who is this fool who sits above your stove?" Tugarin asked.

"He is no fool," the prince replied. "He is the great knight Alesha."

The next moment Tugarin stood up and threw his knife at Alesha. However, the young man grabbed the knife's handle before it could strike him and threw the knife to the floor. Then Tugarin grunted and stormed out of the palace.

Alesha was not finished with Tugarin. The next day Alesha set out to find the giant. On his way, Alesha met a holy man who wore a priest's hat and a dark robe. He carried a heavy staff.

"Father," Alesha said to the man, "would you trade your clothes and staff with me?"

The holy man thought for a moment and then agreed. In his heart, he knew that Alesha's reasons were noble. Alesha was hoping to trick the monster by disguising himself in different clothes.

After many more days of travel, Alesha saw the giant flying above him. Tugarin had made himself a pair of paper wings. He was flying high in the sky on the back of a great golden horse.

"Dear God," Alesha prayed very softly,

"please make the rains come."

The rains came quickly and very hard. Tugarin's paper wings got wet, and he started to fall to earth. He could see Alesha below him. The priest's clothes didn't fool this clever giant.

"Now," Tugarin thought as he fell toward the ground, "I will crush this fool with my horse's hooves."

When Tugarin reached him, Alesha hid under the horse's long, golden mane. Tugarin could not see him. When Tugarin looked the other way, Alesha took a mighty swing with the priest's staff and knocked Tugarin's head off. Tugarin's horse quickly galloped off into the woods. Alesha traveled back to the prince's palace.

"Hail, Prince Vladimir," Alesha said when he arrived at the palace. "I have slain the giant Tugarin. You will never find him at your dinner table again!"

1. *Why did Alesha sit on the ledge above the stove?*
2. *Why didn't the prince tell Turgarin to leave his table?*
3. *Why did Tugarin fall to earth?*

The Forest Creatures

In Russian mythology, many different creatures live in the forest. One of them is the leshii *who looks like an old man and has tangled hair and a long beard. His skin is rough, and he is covered with shaggy hair. The leshii sometimes kidnaps young children. Sometimes the leshii rewards people who performed services for him or helped him in some other way. This story was told by Russian peasants who lived near the forest.*

There was once a young tailor who traveled across the land in search of work. For many months, however, the tailor found no work. He was very unhappy and began to fear that soon he would have no money left for food.

The tailor met a stranger on the street and explained why he was so unhappy. "I need money badly," the tailor told the man. "I would sew for the leshii himself if he asked."

"Well, come to my house," the stranger replied. "I need to have a blanket sewn from sheepskins."

The tailor was delighted to finally get

work. He followed the man to a large house. There he met the stranger's wife.

The wife found out that the tailor was going to sew the sheepskin blanket.

"My husband wants a very special blanket," the wife said to the tailor. "Let me warn you that many other tailors have made my husband angry because of their poor work. If you do a good job for him, he will reward you."

Then the husband gave the tailor a large stack of skins. The tailor laid out the skins and began his sewing.

Soon the tailor had finished a beautiful sheepskin blanket. The stranger liked the blanket very much. He asked the tailor to make a coat and boots for his young son. When the coat and boots were finished, the stranger was again very pleased.

During the months to come, the tailor was kept very busy making hats, mittens, and jackets for the stranger's family. Then it came time for the tailor to be paid.

"My husband will be paying you soon," the wife told the tailor. "When he asks you how much he owes you, just tell him that he knows the value of your work."

When the husband did ask, the tailor said

exactly what the wife had told him to say.

"I know a beautiful woman who has agreed to be your wife," the stranger said. He gave the tailor the hand of the loveliest young woman the tailor had ever seen.

"I will give you a carriage with horses and fifty rubles to start your new married life," the stranger continued. Just then there appeared a golden carriage, drawn by two white horses. In the carriage, the tailor found a bag with the fifty rubles inside.

The tailor rode into town with the woman to arrange their wedding. On his way to the church, the tailor passed the town mayor on the street.

"Those are my horses!" the mayor yelled. "Stop, thief!"

"These horses were payment for my work," the tailor said. "If only the man who gave them to me were here, I could prove it to you."

Suddenly the stranger appeared from out of nowhere. He was the leshii.

"You know your horses, but don't you know your own daughter?" the leshii asked the mayor. "I stole her when she was a baby, along with your horses and much of your wealth. This man is to be your son-in-law."

Then the leshii disappeared as quickly as he had come. The mayor was overjoyed to have his daughter back. He hugged her and rewarded the tailor for rescuing his daughter. Then the mayor rode with his daughter and the tailor to the church where they were to be married.

1. *In Russian mythology, who is the leshii?*
2. *How did the leshii pay the tailor?*
3. *How did the mayor find his lost daughter?*

Sun, Frost, and Wind

In many Russian stories, the wind and other powers of nature appear in human form. These powers of nature often compete with one another. In this story, the sun, the frost, and the wind are men. Each of them wants to be more important than the other two.

One autumn day a peasant was walking home. He was returning from a hard day of harvesting. Three men approached the peasant. They were Sun, Frost, and Wind. The peasant stopped, tipped his hat, and bowed to the men.

"Which one of us are you bowing to?" the first man asked.

"Well," the peasant replied, "first I must know who all of you are."

The first man, who was very round and red, said, "I am Sun."

The second man was much thinner and had bushy, white eyebrows. He said, "I am Frost."

The third man had messy hair, ragged clothes, and a swollen face. He was the meanest looking one of the three. "I am

Wind," he answered forcefully.

The peasant was afraid of Wind. So he replied, "Of course I was bowing to His Highness the Wind."

Sun and Frost were very angry when they heard the peasant's words. Sun said he might burn the peasant to ashes. Frost said he might freeze the peasant's ears off. However, Wind laughed and told the peasant that he would protect him.

When the peasant returned home, he remembered the threats made by Sun and Frost. Since summer had passed, the peasant was not afraid of Sun. He was worried about Frost, though, since winter was near.

When winter came, the peasant wanted to stay inside to avoid Frost. The peasant could not stay inside all the time, though. He had to go to the forest to chop firewood.

One day Frost saw the peasant working. Frost started to freeze the peasant's face and his hands and toes. The peasant chopped faster and faster, and he became very hot. He rushed to stack the wood, and he got hotter and hotter. Then he ran until he got so hot that old Frost simply could not freeze him.

"Thank you, Frost," the peasant said pleasantly. "You helped me get my work done quicker than ever before." Frost did not try to freeze the peasant again.

So far, the peasant had not needed Wind to protect him during the winter.

When spring came, the peasant began to plow his fields. Then he planted his crops.

"Now I'll have my chance," Sun said. Then Sun started to burn the peasant and the new crops he had planted. The peasant was not able to hide from Sun.

It was time for Wind to help. Wind blew strong breezes over the peasant to cool him. Then he chased a cloud over the land and brought a cool, gentle rain.

"I told you I would help," Wind exclaimed. "You bowed to me, and I have protected you."

Sun had to admit that he could not burn the peasant. Wind had shown that he could keep that from happening. Frost admitted, too, that Wind was very strong.

From that time on, Sun and Frost did not bother the peasant. They did not try to cause him any harm at all.

1. *What did the peasant do that made Sun and Frost angry?*
2. *How did Frost help the peasant?*
3. *How did Wind help the peasant?*

Father Frost

Russia is a country of fierce snowstorms and bitter cold. Morozko, sometimes called Father Frost, treats people differently depending on how they treat him.

There once lived an old man and an old woman who had three daughters. The man had been married once before. The oldest daughter, Marfusha, was the child of his first marriage.

The old woman didn't like her stepdaughter. She would often yell at her. She made her do all the hard work around the house.

Marfusha's father had been ill and could not defend his daughter. Marfusha fed the animals, pumped water from the well, and chopped firewood. She did all of the sewing and cleaning. However, none of the work she did ever pleased her stepmother.

Marfusha never complained. Still, no matter what she did for them, her stepmother and stepsisters were never kind to her.

Years passed and the girls grew up. The

man began to think of finding husbands for his daughters. Then the woman got an idea.

"I think that Marfusha should marry first," the woman said to her husband. "Tomorrow you must take her into the forest to wait for her husband."

The man knew that Morozko, or Father Frost, lived in the forest. If Morozko didn't help her in a short while, Marfusha would freeze to death. The man was too weak to speak up for his daughter.

"Pack up all your things, Marfusha," the old woman said. "Tomorrow your father will take you to meet your husband."

Marfusha was very excited. She didn't know anything about Morozko. She packed her things and slept very soundly that night. In the morning, she wore her finest dress to meet her husband.

"Now hurry up," the woman yelled to Marfusha. Then to her husband she said, "Take her deep into the forest to the largest of all the fir trees. There Morozko will come for her as night falls. He will make a good husband for Marfusha."

Sadly the man put Marfusha's things in his sleigh. He told Marfusha to put on her warmest coat. They rode off together and after a long while came to the largest fir tree in the forest.

"Sit here, my dear daughter, beneath this tree," Marfusha's father said. "Wait here for your husband. When he comes for you, be as pleasant as you can." Then the man rode off in the sleigh to return home.

Marfusha sat in the cold snow under the tree. She felt like crying, but she knew that tears would only make her feel colder. Suddenly she began to hear a snapping and cracking in the branches of the trees. It was Morozko, hopping from tree to tree.

When Morozko came to the top of the tree Marfusha was sitting under, he spoke gently to her.

"Are you warm down there, my girl?" he asked.

"Oh, yes, kind sir, I am very warm," she replied. She tried not to show how much she was shaking.

Morozko slowly climbed down the tree.

"Are you still warm, my dear?" he asked.

"Oh, yes, I am just fine," Marfusha replied, although she was getting even colder.

Then Morozko got closer and closer until the girl was almost completely frozen.

"And now? Are you cold yet?" he asked.

"Oh, no," Marfusha replied, "I am still quite warm, thank you."

At last Morozko felt so sorry for her that he wrapped her in warm blankets. She smiled and told him how very nice he was.

The next morning the old woman told her husband to ride back out to the forest.

"See how our Marfusha is doing," the old woman laughed.

When he got there, the man found, to his surprise, that Marfusha was still alive. She was wearing a beautiful fur coat and a gleaming silk scarf around her head. Beside her, stood a chest full of the finest jewels. The man loaded all of Marfusha's presents onto the sleigh and happily drove back home with her.

The old woman was amazed to see that Marfusha was still alive. She was envious of all the riches Morozko had given to her stepdaughter.

After a short while, the old woman said to her husband, "I think it's time you take my daughters to be married."

The next morning the woman dressed her daughters in their finest dresses and warmest coats.

Marfusha

Her husband drove them to the forest and left them at the same tall fir tree. The two sisters looked at each other, and then they started to laugh.

"Surely mother has lost her senses, sending us way out here to meet our husbands," one of them said.

The sisters' sheepskin coats did not keep them warm for very long. Soon they started complaining and fighting with each other.

"I wish those husbands would hurry up." "I'm freezing," one sister said.

"Surely if just one man appears, he will choose me over you," said the other sister.

"Is that so?" the first replied. "Well, we will see about that, won't we?"

Morozko heard what the girls were saying and nipped their fingers with frost. The sisters complained all the more. They blew on their fingers to keep them warm as Morozko moved closer. He rested above them in the huge tree and spoke.

"Are you warm down there, my girls?" he asked.

"This cold is awful," one sister said.

"We have been waiting for our husbands to come, but the horrible beasts haven't come yet," the other said. "We are freezing."

Morozko moved closer down the tree to them.

"Are you warm down there, girls?" he asked.

"Can't you see we're almost frozen?" one sister replied.

Morozko came even closer and made them colder. Then he asked them once more, "Are you warm now, girls?" This time the sisters swore at him and told him to leave them alone.

Morozko left them alone. By morning the two girls had frozen to death.

The old woman sent her husband to bring back her daughters. He rushed off in the sleigh and drove to the tall fir tree. There he found both of the girls dead. He rolled them into a fur blanket and took them home.

The old woman saw her husband coming from a distance and ran to meet him. She looked in the sleigh and saw her daughters lying dead.

"You have killed my lovely daughters," the wife yelled at her husband. Then she swung at him with a poker from the fire.

"I have had enough from you, foolish old woman," the husband said. "It was your greed that killed them, not me. You told me to take them there."

The old woman continued to yell at her husband for a long while. In time, however, the wife asked Marfusha for her forgiveness. Later Marfusha met a neighbor's handsome son and they were married in a warm chapel.

The old man would often tell stories of Morozko to his grandchildren. Marufusha's stepmother never caused any problems for her again.

1. *What did Marfusha say when Morozko asked her about the cold?*
2. *What did Morozko give Marfusha?*
3. *What happened to Marfusha's sisters?*

The Three Suitors

In this Russian tale, the sun and the moon appear as living beings. A farmer who meets up with them goes through some humorous adventures. He finally decides that being himself is the best way to be.

One day a farmer was walking home with a pail of grain when he tripped and fell. The grain flew all over the ground. It was late, and the farmer feared that he couldn't pick up all the grain before dark.

"Red Raven," he called toward the sky, "please come down and help me."

Soon the beautiful Red Raven swooped down to the farmer's side.

"Farmer, you have three daughters. Am I right?" the bird asked.

"Yes, you are right," the farmer replied, "but why do you ask?"

"I will help you if you let me marry your youngest daughter," Red Raven replied.

The farmer agreed. However, now it was too dark for them to pick up the grain.

"Moon," the farmer called, "light up the sky so we can see my grain."

"I will shine for you if you let me marry your second oldest daughter," Moon said.

Again the farmer agreed, and Moon shone brightly. However, now the farmer was too cold to pick up the grain.

"Bright Sun, please warm me," the farmer begged.

"I will warm you if you let me marry your oldest daughter," Bright Sun answered.

The farmer agreed once more, and Bright Sun warmed the farmer. Then the farmer gathered his grain with the help of Red Raven, Moon, and Bright Sun. When he had finished, he made his long journey home. When he got there, he found that his three daughters had vanished that very night. They had already gone to their husbands.

Soon the farmer missed his daughters, so he decided to visit them.

First, the farmer visited the home of Bright Sun. His oldest daughter met him at the door.

"Father, you look hungry," she said. "I will make some pancakes." She put some batter in a pan and placed it on her husband's head to cook.

Soon the pancakes were done, and the farmer ate his fill. He returned to his wife and told her about his visit.

"Now I want you to make me some pancakes," he said. His wife put some batter in a pan. Then her husband told her to put the pan on the top of his head. The pancakes did not cook, and the batter spilled all over the farmer.

Next, the farmer went to visit his second daughter. Soon he arrived at the home of Moon.

"Father, you need a bath," his daughter said to the dusty farmer. She led him into a very dark bathhouse.

"I can't bathe in here. It's too dark," the farmer told her. All of a sudden, Moon put his hand through a crack in the wall and the bathhouse became very bright. The farmer had a fine bath and returned home to tell his wife about his visit.

"Let's have a bath," the farmer said to his wife, leading her to their own bathhouse.

"Farmer," the wife said, "we can't have a bath in here. It's too dark." Then the farmer put his hand through a crack in the wall, but the bathhouse still stayed very dark. The farmer and his wife did not have a bath. As they walked out, they both slipped on soap and bumped their heads.

Later the farmer went to the home of Red Raven to see his youngest daughter. "Where is your husband?" the farmer asked his youngest daughter when he arrived.

"Oh, he is fast asleep on his perch," the youngest daughter said. She led the farmer to a tree branch where Red Raven sat sleeping. The farmer was tired and climbed up beside Red Raven. The farmer slept while leaning against Red Raven. The next day, after a fine rest, the farmer went home and told his wife about his visit.

"Why don't we perch in a tree to sleep?" he asked his wife.

"Not me!" she replied. "I will sleep in my bed as always!"

The farmer climbed onto a tree branch and fell asleep. However, as soon as he had dozed off, he fell to the ground. The bump on his head from this fall was even bigger than the bump from the bathhouse fall.

From that night on, the farmer never again tried to act like his daughters' husbands.

1. *Why did the farmer want Red Raven to help him?*
2. *Why did Red Raven, Moon, and Bright Sun agree to help the farmer?*
3. *How did the oldest daughter cook pancakes?*

Prince Ivan and the Sun's Sister

In Russian stories, witches appear in some very unusual places. In this story, a young man uses magical gifts to outsmart an evil witch who is a member of his own family.

A young man who was a tsar's son was unable to speak. One night this young man, named Ivan, heard a voice while he was sleeping. The voice told him that his mother was about to give birth to a witch. This witch would eat him and his parents shortly after she was born. The voice told him to run away to a safe place.

The next morning Ivan was so afraid that he went to his father and begged for a horse. Ivan's father, the tsar, was shocked to hear his son speak. So he gave Ivan the horse at once. Ivan wanted to search for a safe place where the witch couldn't find him.

Ivan traveled until he met two old women sewing. He asked if he could stay with them.

"We will die as soon as our needles are gone," the women said. Ivan saw that they had only a very few needles left, so he kept on riding.

Next Ivan came to a man named Pull Up Oak. He asked if he could stay with him.

"I will die as soon as I finish pulling these oak trees out of the ground," Pull Up Oak said. Ivan knew that the job would not take the man very long, so he rode on.

Ivan came to another man, named Overturn Mountain. Ivan asked if he could stay with him.

"As soon as I overturn these mountains, I will die," said Overturn Mountain. By now the young man was very tired and very disappointed, but he continued on his way.

Ivan was just about to give up hope when he came to the home of the sun's sister. She welcomed him into her home as if he were her own son.

Ivan lived happily with the sun's sister, but he often thought of the family he had left behind. One day he said to the sun's sister, "I want to find out what happened to my family."

The sun's sister understood that Ivan had to leave. She gave him four gifts—a comb, a brush, and two red apples.

"Each of these gifts has a magical power," she said. "You will know what those powers are when you need them."

Ivan began his journey. On the road back home, Ivan once again met Overturn Mountain. He had only one mountain left to overturn. Ivan dropped his brush, and thousands of high mountains rose from the earth.

Next he met Pull Up Oak, who had only one tree left in the ground. Then Ivan dropped his comb, and new forests with tall trees sprang up.

When Ivan met the two old women sewing, he gave each of them a red apple. They ate the apples and became young again. The women were very grateful to Ivan and gave him a magic scarf.

When Ivan reached the door of his parents' house, he met his sister. She didn't look like a witch at all. She smiled and told Ivan to have a seat while she looked for their parents. As Ivan waited, a little mouse appeared.

"She's lying to you, Ivan," the mouse warned. "She killed your parents long ago. Now she is getting ready to kill you, too!"

Ivan ran out of the house for his life. His sister ran after him.

Ivan soon reached a clearing in the woods. His sister was close behind. Ivan

Ivan is saved from the witch

dropped the magic scarf. Suddenly a vast lake spread out between them. Ivan's sister swam the lake while Ivan ran ahead.

The witch was catching up with Ivan when Pull Up Oak stopped her. He blocked her path with a great pile of oak trees.

The sister climbed over the trees. Once again she started to catch up with Ivan. Then Overturn Mountain laid two great mountains in her path. The witch slowed down at first but then ran faster and soon almost caught up with her brother.

Ivan could see the home of the sun's sister in the distance. Ivan was on a bridge to the sun's sister's home when he heard the witch speak.

"I have trapped you now, brother Ivan," the witch said. Then she put one of her huge witch feet on the end of the bridge.

The witch's big foot came down with such a heavy force that Ivan flew high into the air. He landed safely inside the home of the sun's sister.

The sun's sister was very happy to see Ivan back in her home at last. She vowed to protect him forever. The witch sister is still roaming the country and trying to think of a way to get her brother.

1. *What made Ivan speak?*
2. *When Ivan first met Pull Up Oak, what did the man tell him?*
3. *Why did the two old women give Ivan the magic scarf?*

The Magic Acorn

Many Russians long ago lived in small wooden houses called izbas. *These simple buildings had a large main room, where the whole family lived. Another smaller room was used to store food and other things. The people in this story have an adventure without even having to leave their izba.*

There once lived an old couple. They were so poor that they had to gather acorns in the forest for food. One day an acorn rolled into the cellar beneath their izba. The acorn put down roots and grew into a little tree. Soon it reached the floor of their izba. The old woman cut a hole in the floor so that the tree could keep growing.

"Some day we'll be able to eat acorns from the tree right here in our own izba!" she exclaimed.

The tree grew bigger and bigger, so the old man cut a hole in the roof. In just a few more days, it had become a mighty oak tree.

The old man climbed to the top of the tree to collect the acorns. When he got to the top, he found a beautiful rooster with a golden comb and a hand mill for grinding corn. He gently picked up the rooster and the hand mill and brought them down into the izba.

The old woman quickly tried out the hand mill. No sooner had she turned the handle than pancakes came tumbling out. The old couple ate their fill. They were so happy to be eating something other than acorns.

Many weeks later, a lord who was passing by stopped and asked the couple for something to eat.

"Would you like some fine pancakes?" the old woman asked. Then she turned the handle of the mill. The lord ate pancakes until he was almost ready to burst.

"I want to buy your mill," the lord said to the old couple.

"Oh, we can't sell it," the couple said.

The lord was an evil man and just picked up the mill and took it with him.

"What can we do?" the old man asked. "He is a rich lord, and we are but lowly peasants. If we go after him, surely we will end up in prison."

The old couple were very angry. All of a sudden, the rooster spoke to them.

"Do not worry, my friends," the rooster crowed. "I will get the mill back for you."

The rooster flew to the lord's house and perched outside a window. "Coo-cuckoo!" the rooster crowed loudly. "Give us back our magic mill!"

The lord heard the rooster and told his butler to throw the bird into the well. The butler followed the lord's orders.

"My good beak! My good beak!" the rooster cried from the well. "Drink up all the water." Then the rooster's own beak drank up all the water in the well. The rooster flew up and out of the well. This time he flew right into the lord's kitchen.

"Coo-cuckoo!" the rooster cried. "Give us back our magic mill."

The lord ordered the cook to throw the rooster in the fire beneath the oven. The cook did as he was told. From inside the fire, the rooster cried out again.

"My good beak! My good beak! Pour out the water!" he crowed. All of the well water poured from his beak and put out the fire. It also flooded the whole kitchen.

Then the rooster flew into the dining room and sat down in the middle of the lord's table. "Coo-cuckoo!" the rooster crowed. "Give us back our magic mill!"

All the lord's guests screamed and ran out

of the room. The lord ran after his guests, trying to get them to come back. While he was out of the house, the rooster grabbed the mill and flew away back to the old couple.

From that day on, the old couple lived very happily. They kept their rooster and their hand mill safe in their izba with the oak tree in it.

1. *What did the old man find at the top of the oak tree?*
2. *What did the rooster do after the lord had him thrown in the well?*
3. *Why did the couple want the mill back?*

The Apple in the Saucer

Some kind and helpful characters in Russian legends are treated unjustly or cruelly. Usually these characters possess something that someone else desires. The unfair treatment is always punished in some way. In this story, two sisters are jealous of their younger sister.

There once lived an old Russian couple who had three daughters. The two older daughters never did any work. They always wore pretty clothes. The youngest daughter did all the work in the house. She didn't care about fancy clothes. She was very shy, and she didn't talk very much. Her parents and sisters called her Little Simple One.

One day the father was going to the market to sell his crops. He asked his daughters what presents he could bring back for them. The two oldest asked for bolts of colored cloth to make new dresses.

"What about you, Little Simple One?" the father asked. "What would you like me to bring back for you?"

"I want a silver saucer and a shiny red apple," she replied.

"What on earth for?" her mother asked.

"Yesterday," Little Simple One said, "I gave an old beggar a loaf of bread. She told me how to make magic."

"You are very strange," said the two sisters. They laughed at her, as they had so many times before.

That night their father returned from the market. The two older daughters were excited about making new dresses from the cloth he had brought. Then they watched Little Simple One to see what she would do with the saucer and the apple.

Little Simple One sat in a corner and began to repeat these words:

"Roll in the saucer, apple roll,
wonderful places show.
Take me to cities and mountains
and oceans, wherever
your light may go."

The apple rolled over the saucer, and countless sights appeared to Little Simple One. She saw ships sailing on the seas and high mountain ranges. She saw cities with gleaming towers and skies filled with suns and stars and moons.

Little Simple One's sisters were jealous. They wanted the saucer and the apple, but

Wonderful sights appear

she would not trade them for anything. Then the sisters got an idea.

"Let's all go to the forest to pick wild berries," one of them said. The three sisters strolled off with their berry baskets. Little Simple One had left the saucer and the apple with her father.

When the three sisters got to the forest, the wicked sisters saw a shovel lying near the wild berries. They picked up the shovel and hit Little Simple One on the head, killing her. The sisters then buried her on a little hill under a small tree.

"Now we will have that saucer and apple," one wicked sister said to the other.

The two sisters returned home. They told their father that Little Simple One had been eaten by wolves. Their father was very sad. In honor of his daughter, he locked the saucer and the apple in a small wooden box.

A few days later, a shepherd was tending his sheep near the berry patch. There he found a little hill covered with red and blue flowers. In the middle of the flowers was a tiny tree.

The shepherd broke a little reed off the tree to make a musical pipe. Much to his surprise, the little pipe began playing on its own. Then it started to speak.

"Toot, toot, toot, little tune," the pipe played. "Make my father smile, though my sisters have killed me for a silver saucer and an apple."

The shepherd recognized the voice. He ran to get Little Simple One's father. Then the shepherd brought the old man to the little hill.

Again the little pipe played on its own.

"Dear father," it played, "my own two sisters killed me for the silver saucer and the apple. Now only water from the royal well can bring me back to life."

The father hurried home to talk to his other daughters. They admitted killing their sister. The father tied their hands together and locked them in the cellar.

Then the father went to visit the tsar. After hearing the father's story, the tsar let him draw water from the royal well.

"When your daughter comes back to life," said the tsar, "bring her to see me. Also bring the two young women who killed her. I want to see that silver saucer with the shiny apple, too."

The father agreed and hurried back to the forest with the bottle of water. He spilled a few drops of the water on the little hill. His Little Simple One suddenly rose from the earth. She was alive once again.

As he had promised the tsar, the father returned to the royal palace with his three daughters. The tsar asked Little Simple One to show him the saucer and the apple.

Standing before the tsar, Little Simple One rolled the apple over the silver saucer. The tsar saw cities and mountains and skies full of stars. He saw flags and fireworks and thousands of soldiers in brightly colored uniforms. He saw sailing ships and great whales and jungles with swinging apes. Then he heard thunder. Smoke rose from the little plate and everything disappeared. The apple needed time to rest.

Little Simple One began to cry. Then she fell to her knees at the tsar's feet.

"Your Majesty," she begged, "keep my saucer and my apple, but do not punish my sisters for what they have done."

The tsar forgave the wicked sisters. With a broad smile, he took Little Simple One by the hand.

"Your kindness will be rewarded," the tsar said. "Will you be my wife and help me rule my kingdom?"

Little Simple One agreed to marry the tsar. Every city in the land sent a silver saucer of food to their wedding feast. The two sisters never did another wicked thing again.

1. *What could the silver saucer and the apple do?*
2. *What did the father do to the two wicked sisters when he found out they had killed Little Simple One?*
3. *What did Little Simple One ask the tsar to do to her sisters?*

The Snake Princess

Long ago many Russians feared snakes. Some of them, however, honored snakes and brought them offerings of food. Some people believed that a dried snake skin could lower a person's fever. There are many legends in which snakes appear. In this story, the snake is really a princess.

One day a cossack, or soldier, was riding his horse in a dark forest. He came upon a large haystack, lay down beside it, and lit his pipe. He was careless with the flame and caught the hay on fire. He feared that he would be burned and jumped up quickly.

Soon the whole forest lit up. The cossack saw a lovely young woman standing in the middle of the fire.

"Please save me, cossack," she screamed.

"I would if I could," he replied, "but I can't reach you through the fire."

"Put your sword through the fire, and I will crawl out on it," the woman called.

The cossack did as she said. The young woman turned into a snake and coiled around the sword and up the cossack's arm.

The snake princess

Then she wrapped herself around his neck.

"Don't be afraid," the snake said. "Carry me like this for seven years until you find the land of tin. Then stay there for another seven years. You will one day find true happiness."

The cossack was very confused. He got on his horse and rode off, with the snake still wrapped around his neck.

The cossack traveled for seven years until he reached a high mountain. On top of the mountain stood a palace made of tin. The cossack rode up the mountain and into the courtyard of the palace.

Suddenly the snake leapt from his neck to the ground. Once again she became a young woman. Then she disappeared.

The cossack was quite sure the young woman would return. He put his horse in a stable. Then he went into the palace.

There he saw silver and gold objects and fine paintings everywhere. He was startled to see himself in many huge mirrors.

"What an odd place this is," he thought to himself. "There are so many beautiful things everywhere, but there are no people. Worse than that, there is no food!"

At that very instant, a great banquet table appeared, covered with all kinds of food. The cossack sat down and ate until he was full. At the same time, a great wall rose around the palace, trapping the cossack inside.

Many years passed. The cossack always had plenty of food to eat. Nevertheless, he grew very lonely and very sad.

"This is a beautiful place," he exclaimed one day, "but I don't want to live all alone forever."

The next morning the cossack looked out the window and saw his horse saddled and waiting for him. He rushed out to mount the horse. Then he saw the lovely young woman. Over the years, the cossack had thought of her as the snake princess.

"Good morning, cossack," the woman said. "Your seven years in the tin palace are over. I thank you for saving my life. You should know that I am the daughter of a king. Years ago I was taken from my home by an evil man named Koschei the Deathless. When I refused to marry him, he turned me into a snake. Now, let's hurry to my home."

The cossack mounted his horse and put the snake princess in front of him. The great wall disappeared into the earth, and the couple rode off.

"If my father offers you great riches," the snake princess said to the cossack, "refuse them. Tell him you want only the barrel from the palace cellar."

"A barrel?" the cossack asked.

"Yes," the snake princess replied. "It is a special barrel. If you roll it in front of you, you will have whatever your heart desires."

At last the couple arrived at the palace of the snake princess's father. The king thanked the cossack for returning his daughter. He placed large sacks of gold and jewels before the cossack.

"Your Majesty," the cossack said, "all I want is the barrel from your cellar."

"You ask a lot," the king replied. "I cherish my daughter so much, though, that I will give it to you gladly."

The cossack said good-bye to the snake princess and her father. Then he took the barrel and set off to see the world.

After many days of travel, the cossack met an old man.

"Please, kind fellow, won't you give me something to eat?" the old man asked.

The cossack got down off his horse and rolled the barrel in front of him. A grand palace appeared. The cossack took the old man into the dining room of the palace, and they ate until morning. The old man was very grateful to his new friend, who explained the secret power of the barrel.

"Would you trade the barrel for my sword?" the old man asked.

"What?" The cossack replied. "You must be joking."

"This is a very special sword," the old man explained. "It fights battles all by itself."

The cossack was curious but was not sure if he wanted to trade. Then the old man took the cossack out to the forest. He waved the sword in the air. Then he ordered it to cut down a grove of trees. In an instant, the job was done.

"Do you see what I mean?" the old man asked. "With a wave of this sword, you can dash any enemy to pieces."

The cossack traded the barrel for the sword and rode off in search of new adventures. He stopped in a peasant village, where he met another traveler. This man told him that the kingdom of the snake princess's father was under attack.

The cossack mounted his horse and sped back to the snake princess and her father. As he neared their palace, he could see thousands of soldiers attacking it.

"Great sword of mine," he shouted, waving the sword in the air, "dash those armies to the ground."

The sword leapt from his hand and began battling soldier after soldier. Within an hour, the fighting was over. The King and his daughter, the snake princess, had been saved.

1. *How did the cossack rescue the young woman from the fire?*
2. *What kept the cossack in the tin palace?*
3. *How did the cossack get the magic sword?*

The Wizard

Volkh is a well-known wizard and hunter in Russian mythology. He has special powers, such as superhuman strength and the ability to change into animal form.

Many years ago a young princess named Marfa gave birth to a beautiful baby boy. When he was born, the sky lit up and the sea roared. An earthquake was felt throughout the land. Animals from all over the world found places to hide. Fish in the seas swam down deep in the waters. This was no ordinary baby.

The princess named her baby Volkh. When he was only one hour old, Volkh spoke to his mother in a voice as loud as thunder.

"Noble Mother Marfa," he said, "do not dress me in the clothes of a child. Put me into a coat of steel armor. Put a great helmet on my head and a sword in my hand."

His mother did as he had asked.

By the time he was seven years old, Volkh could read and write. A few years later he found that he could change shapes. Volkh could become a falcon, a wolf, or anything else.

When Volkh was twelve years old, he began to gather an army around him. By the time he was fifteen, he had an army of seven thousand soldiers, all of his own age. Volkh's mother realized that her son was a wizard.

Volkh had heard that the king of India was preparing to attack Russia. Within a week, Volkh began marching his great army into India. Sometimes he became a wolf to catch animals to feed his troops. At other times, he turned himself into a falcon to find birds and fish for his men.

As his army neared the king's palace, Volkh feared for the safety of his soldiers.

"I must become a wild ox and run before you," Volkh told his army. "In that way I can learn this king's plan." In an instant, he turned into a wild ox with golden horns. He raced like the wind toward the king's palace.

Volkh turned himself into a falcon when he reached the palace. Then he flew high into the air, landing on a window ledge outside the king's chamber. He saw the king and a beautiful woman who was crying.

"Are you ready to become my wife?" the king asked.

"I have told you before, and I will tell you again," the woman replied, "never!" Then she continued, "Tell me, king, are you afraid of this Volkh the Wizard and his army?"

"No, I should say not!" the king replied.

"Then why have you filled your palace with weapons for fighting a war?" she asked. The king did not answer.

Volkh quickly turned himself into a fox. He scampered through every room in the great palace until he found the king's weapons. Then, with his sharp teeth, he chewed through bowstrings and broke arrows. He buried thousands of guns in the soft earth of the palace yard. Then he turned himself into a falcon and flew back to his army waiting in the woods.

"It is time for us to march on India," Volkh told his men. The army marched up to the thick stone wall around the palace. There were many guards at the gates. Volkh wondered how his army might get inside without being seen. Then he noticed some small cracks in the stone wall.

Volkh had an idea and turned himself and all his men into tiny ants. They crawled through the cracks in the wall to the other side. Then Volkh and his men became soldiers once again.

"Roam the city, my men, and defeat

everyone you see," Volkh told them. "Spare no one except those women that you want to marry."

Volkh himself stormed into the king's palace. With one kick of his massive foot, he broke down the steel gate. He picked up the king, spun him high in the air, and smashed him down on the stone floor. When the king hit the floor, he broke into millions of tiny pieces. Volkh threw these pieces far out into the sky, where they became stars.

The woman who had been held prisoner by the evil king was grateful to Volkh. She agreed to be his wife. His men and their brides-to-be joined them in the palace. They were all married in the largest wedding ever known in Russia.

1. *How old was Volkh when he spoke to his mother?*
2. *What were some of the things Volkh turned himself into?*
3. *What finally happened to the king?*

The Magic Doll

Baba Yaga appears as both a good witch and a bad witch in Russian folk tales. Almost always she lives in a little hut built on chickens' legs that spins in the wind. Baba Yaga is very old and looks almost like a skeleton. She has a long pointed nose, and her teeth are very sharp. Baba Yaga is feared most because she eats people and kidnaps children.

A merchant had one daughter named Vasilisa the Beautiful. She was eight years old when her mother died.

Before she died, the girl's mother had given her a very special doll. When Vasilisa fed this doll, it would give her words of wisdom and other kinds of help.

Years later, the merchant married a widow with two daughters. The new stepmother and stepsisters were very jealous of Vasilisa. They made her do all the hard work both indoors and out. They thought that so much work would make her ugly, but they were wrong.

As Vasilisa became more and more beautiful, her stepmother and stepsisters hated her even more. Whenever she felt sad, Vasilisa would feed her magic doll. Then the doll would talk to her. Often the doll even helped her with her work. Without the doll, Vasilisa could not have survived.

One day the merchant had to go away for a long time.

"Now we shall see about Vasilisa," the stepmother said to the stepsisters.

That night Vasilisa's stepmother opened the door to their house just as a very strong wind was blowing. The wind blew out all the candles as the stepsisters sat sewing.

"How can we sew our lovely dresses with no light?" one stepsister asked.

"We have no fire to light the candles," the stepmother said. "Vasilisa, you will have to travel deep into the forest to Baba Yaga to get us some new fire."

Vasilisa knew what this meant. Baba Yaga was a wicked witch who ate people. Sadly Vasilisa put on her coat. She put her doll in her pocket and left for the witch's hut.

Along the path to the hut, Vasilisa stopped to feed her doll some crumbs of bread.

"Do not worry, my friend," the doll said. "Just keep me with you, and you will be safe." Vasilisa walked all night and all the next day until it became dark again. Then she came to a little hut on tall chickens' legs. Around the hut was a fence made of human bones.

Vasilisa soon heard a loud rumbling through the trees. Then she saw Baba Yaga coming home, riding in a large mortar, which looks like a bowl. She was rowing with a pestle, a club-shaped tool used for grinding things. Baba Yaga stopped at the fence and began to sniff the air.

"I smell a young Russian woman," cackled the witch. "Where is she?"

"I am here," Vasilisa said. "I have come for some fire so that my stepmother can light the candles in our house."

"I see," the witch said. "Maybe I will give you some fire. Maybe I won't. First you must stay and work for me. If you do as you are told, all will be well. If not, you will make many fine suppers for old Baba Yaga." The wicked old witch laughed and frightened Vasilisa very much.

Every morning for a week the witch rode off from her hut. First she told Vasilisa what work had to be done. While the witch was gone, Vasilisa planted and picked and cooked

The witch's mortar and pestle

and cleaned. Her doll talked to her all the while. The doll helped Vasilisa with most of the work.

At the end of the week, Baba Yaga spoke to Vasilisa more kindly than before.

"You are very good," said Baba Yaga. "You have caused me no trouble, and you have worked very hard. I am not going to eat you after all." Then Baba Yaga gave Vasilisa a skull filled with fire and sent her on her way back home.

Vasilisa and her doll hurried home in the glow of the light from the skull. When she got there, Vasilisa's stepmother and stepsisters were shocked. They had been sure that Baba Yaga would eat her.

The stepmother and stepsisters lit their candles while Vasilisa went to bed. The next morning, much to Vasilisa's surprise, she found all three of them burned to ashes. Baba Yaga had given the skull a curse that had killed them.

Vasilisa went to live with a kind old woman while she waited for her father to come back.

The old woman asked Vasilisa to make some linen shirts for the tsar. With the help of her doll, Vasilisa made the loveliest shirts.

When the tsar saw the shirts, he said, "Bring me the one who has made these fine shirts."

The old woman brought Vasilisa to the royal palace. The tsar fell in love with her and asked Vasilisa to marry him.

Vasilisa's father returned shortly. He was very pleased to hear of Vasilisa's good fortune. Soon both he and the kind old woman went to live in the tsar's palace. Vasilisa carried her doll in her pocket every day of her life.

1. *What did Vasilisa do to get her doll to talk to her?*
2. *Why did Vasilisa go to the hut of Baba Yaga?*
3. *How did Vasilisa meet the tsar?*

Pronunciation Guide

Every effort has been made to present native pronunciations of the unusual names in this book. Sometimes experts differed in their opinions, however, or no pronunciation could be found. Also, certain foreign-language sounds were felt to be unpronounceable by today's readers. In these cases, editorial license was exercised in selecting pronunciations.

Key

The letter or letters used to show pronunciation have the following sounds:

a	as in *map* and *glad*
ah	as in *pot* and *cart*
aw	as in *fall* and *lost*
ch	as in *chair* and *child*
e	as in *let* and *care*
ee	as in *feet* and *please*
ey	as in *play* and *face*
g	as in *gold* and *girl*
hy	as in *huge* and *humor*
i	as in *my* and *high*
ih	as in *sit* and *clear*

j	as in *jelly* and *gentle*
k	as in *skill* and *can*
ky	as in *cute*
l	as in *long* and *pull*
my	as in *mule*
ng	as in *sing* and *long*
ny	as in *canyon* and *onion*
o	as in *slow* and *go*
oo	as in *cool* and *move*
ow	as in *cow* and *round*
s	as in *soon* and *cent*
sh	as in *shoe* and *sugar*
th	as in *thin* and *myth*
u	as in *put* and *look*
uh	as in *run* and *up*
y	as in *you* and *yesterday*
z	as in *zoo* and *pairs*

Guide

Capital letters are used to represent stressed syllables. For example, the word *ugly* would be written here as "UHG lee."

Afron: AH fron

Alesha: uh LEE shuh

Baba Yaga: BAH bah yah GAH

cossack: KAH sahk

Dalmat: DAHL maht

Dobrynya: doh BREEN yuh

Elena: yeh LEE nuh

Emilyan: yeh mill YAHN

Finist: FIH nihst

Ivan: ee VAHN

izba: IZZ buh

Koschei: KOH shy

Kuzman: KOOS mahn

leshii: LEH shee

Leontii: lay OHN tee

Marfa: MAHR fuh

Marfusha: mahr FOO shuh

Morozko: muh ROSS koh

Natasha: nah TAHSH uh

Rostov: ROS tahv

Tsar: ZAR

Tugarin: too GAHR in

Vasilisa: vah sih LEE suh

Vasily: vuh SEE lee

Vladimir: vlah DEE meer

Vladislas: vlah DEE slahs

Volkh: VOHLK

Zabava: zuh BAH vuh